Snake

me

Inky

Bee

Name: ....

Class: ....

School: ....

Silent ‹b›

Write some silent ‹b› words in the lamb.

shin
bench
lam_
com_
thum_
crum_s
plum_er
clim_ing
mother
father

mother
_o_h_r
m_t_e_

father
_a_h_r
f_t_e_

Choose a word from the list to fit each sentence.

I _____ my hair every morning.

A baby sheep is called a _____ .

The girls were _____ the tree.

There are cake _____ on the table.

Write the alphabet in capital and lower-case letters.

A a _____ _____ _____ _____

_____ _____ _____ _____

_____ _____ _____ _____

Alphabetical Order

Write the capital letters next to the lower-case letters.

__a __b __c __d __e

__f __g __h __i __j __k __l __m

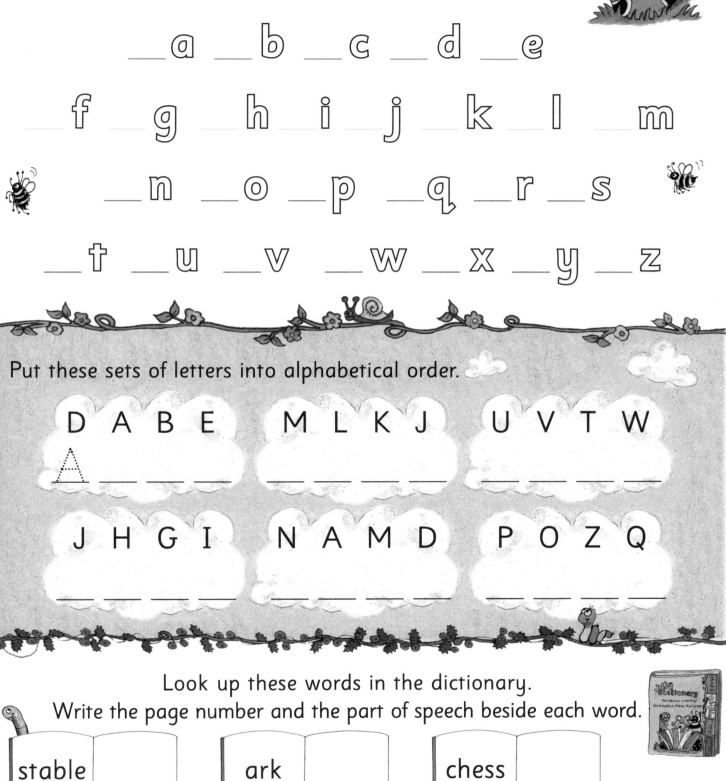

__n __o __p __q __r __s

__t __u __v __w __x __y __z

Put these sets of letters into alphabetical order.

D A B E   M L K J   U V T W

A ___ ___ ___   ___ ___ ___ ___ ___ ___ ___ ___

J H G I   N A M D   P O Z Q

___ ___ ___ ___ ___ ___ ___ ___ ___ ___ ___ ___

Look up these words in the dictionary.
Write the page number and the part of speech beside each word.

stable

ark

chess

zebra

plate

kettle

3

Silent ‹w›

Write some silent ‹w› words in the shipwreck.

chat
cash
_rite
_rist
_reck
_rong
ans_er
s_ordfish
sister
brother

Choose a word from the list to fit each sentence.

She got the answer _____.

Then she got the _____ right.

I must _____ to my pen friend.

He sprained his _____.

sister
_i_t_r
s_s_e_

brother
_r_t_e_
b_o_h_r

Put these words into alphabetical order.

trumpet _____
flute _____
drum _____
harp _____
oboe _____

clown _____
acrobat _____
tent _____
juggler _____

4

Sentence Writing

Write some sentences about the picture.

_____

_____

_____

_____

_____

_____

_____

REMEMBER Each sentence must start with a capital letter and end with a full stop. All sentences must make sense.

song
trunk
_nee
_nit
_now
_nock
_night
pen_nife
grandma
grandpa

Silent ‹k›

Write some silent ‹k› words in the knight's helmet.

Choose a word from the list to fit each sentence.

"Do you _____ the answer?" I asked.

The _____ wore shining armour.

Grandma will _____ a sweater.

Please _____ on the door.

grandma
_ r _ n _ m _
g _ a _ d _ a

grandpa
_ r _ n _ p _
g _ a _ d _ a

Write some sentences about one of your grandparents.
Then draw a picture of him or her.

_____

_____

_____

_____

6

"Speech Marks"

Add the speech marks to these sentences.

Hello Snake, said Inky.

We have been looking for you, buzzed Bee.

Sssss, hissed Snake. Well, here I am.

Snake looked at the letter in Inky's hand. Is that for me? he asked.

Think what the three friends might say next and write the words in the speech bubbles.

Now write out the speech as sentences.

REMEMBER Use speech marks, and explain who speaks which words.

_____

_____

_____

_____

7

this
that
_ _ile
_ _eat
_ _ip
_ _istle
_ _iskers
_ _atever
aunt
uncle

‹wh›

Write some ‹**wh**› words in the whale.

aunt
a _ n _
_ u _ t

uncle
u _ c _ e
_ n _ l _

Choose a word from the list to fit each sentence.

_____ grows in fields.

Becky's cat has white _____.

You can wear _____ you like.

I blew a _____ to start the race.

Put the speech marks in these sentences.

The boy said, I rode my bike.

We like to go swimming, said the children.

Be careful, warned the policeman.

The librarian whispered, Please be quiet.

Questions

What kind of animal would you like to have as a pet?

_____

Why? _____

_____

What? Why? When? Where? Who? Whose? Which? How?

What questions could you ask to find out how to look after it properly?

1._____

2._____

3._____

4._____

Draw a picture of the pet you would like to have.

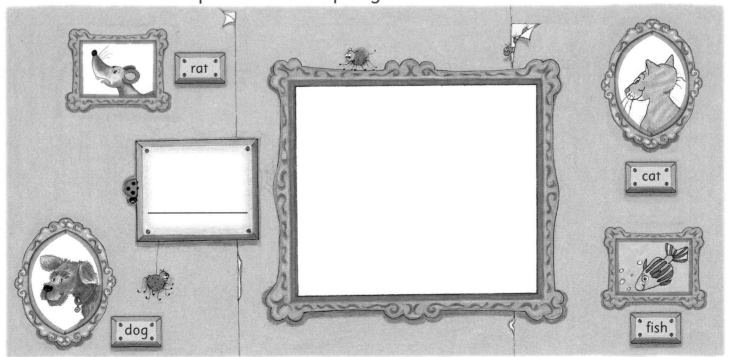

club
flag
_ _one
_ _oto
dol_ _in
ele_ _ant
s_ _ere
al_ _abet
ne_ _ew
niece

‹ph›

Write some ‹ph› words in the elephant.

Choose a word from the list to fit each sentence.

nephew
n_p_e_
_e_h_w

niece
n_e_e
_i_c_

This is a _____ of my baby sister.

We can say the _____.

The _____ swam by the boat.

" _____ me tomorrow," said Tom.

Finish each sentence by adding a question mark or a full stop.

What time do we have to go to bed ☐

An orphan is a child whose mother and father are dead ☐

How old is Grandma ☐

Whose is this photo album ☐

10

Commas in Lists

We use commas to separate words in a list. Add commas to these lists.

Red orange yellow green blue indigo and **violet** are the colours of the rainbow.

Oak elm holly fir beech apple and chestnut are all trees.

On the farm there are cows dogs cats horses sheep and chickens.

REMEMBER Use commas and the word 'and' to separate the words.
Make lists to complete these sentences.

The fruit stall sells _____
_____

My friends are called _____
_____

When it rains I wear _____
_____

My favourite games are _____
_____

At the zoo we saw_____
_____

glad
plum
r _ _ d
h _ _ d
br _ _ d
w _ _ ther
tr _ _ sure
br _ _ kfast
cousin
friend

‹ea› saying the /e/ sound

Write some ‹ea› words in the loaf of bread.

Choose a word from the list to fit each sentence.

The _____ is sunny today.

Dad cooks _____ in the morning.

She found some buried _____.

I have _____ that book already.

cousin
c _ u _ i _
_ o _ s _ n

friend
f _ i _ n _
_ r _ e _ d

Add commas to these lists.

They went out to buy milk butter cheese and bread.

In my garden I grow carrots potatoes tomatoes beans and peas.

Squares circles triangles stars and rectangles are all shapes.

Exclamation Marks!

REMEMBER An exclamation mark shows that the person speaking or writing feels strongly about something.

What might you exclaim if you had these strong feelings?

angry

happy

surprised

afraid

upset

hurt

Fill in the missing punctuation marks.

☐Stop☐☐ shouted the policeman☐

Tina went outside☐ ☐Brr☐ It is freezing☐☐ she said☐

☐Brilliant☐ That is just what I wanted☐☐ exclaimed Seth☐

13

Soft ‹c› saying the /s/ sound

Write some **soft** ‹c› words in the circus tent.

mill
tell
i_e
dan_e
_ity
_ircle
poli_e
_ylinder
January
February

ce
ci
cy

Choose a word from the list to fit each sentence.

A _____ is tube shaped.

I ate a vanilla _____ cream.

The _____ arrested the robber.

We _____ to the music.

January
J _ n _ a _ y
_ a _ u _ r _

February
F _ b _ u _ r _
_ e _ r _ a _ y

Fill in the missing punctuation marks.

◯Stop thief◯◯ shouted the man◯ ◯Call the police◯◯

The police arrived quickly◯ ◯What has been taken◯◯

asked the policeman◯

◯The thief stole two rings◯ a watch◯ a pair of earrings and

a necklace,◯ the man explained◯

14

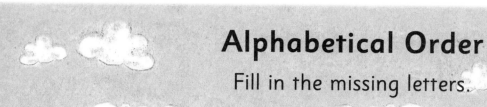

Alphabetical Order

Fill in the missing letters.

A _ C _ _   F G _ I J _ _ M

N _ _ _ Q _ S   T _ _ W _ _ _

Put these words into alphabetical order.

sheep   horse   dog   cow

 **F**   cow _____

swing   bat   bike   toy

 **A**   _____

Tyrone   Sid   Ted   Billy   Tom

_____

 Y   avocado   peach   cherry   orange   plum

_____

chin   clap   cake   cut   coat   crayon   **I**

_____

 S   stop   scar   skin   second   sack   shell

_____

REMEMBER If more than one word starts with the same letter, look at the next letter in each word.

miss
cross
_iant
ma_ic
lar_e
dan_er
oran_e
ve_etable
March
April

Soft ‹g› saying the /j/ sound

Write some **soft ‹g›** words in the vegetables.

ge

gi

gy

Choose a word from the list to fit each sentence.

I ate a bowl of _____ soup.

Then I drank a glass of _____ juice.

Be careful! You are in _____.

The wizard cast a _____ spell.

March
M_r_h
_a_c_

April
A_r_l
_p_i_

Draw a ring around the word that would come first in the dictionary.

amber
acorn

raft
rook

gander
grammar

vowel
vixen

elk
expel

plural
penguin

Proper Nouns

The names of the months are **proper nouns**.
Write them in order on the calendar pages below, and
draw a picture for each month in the space.

REMEMBER Start each month with a capital letter.

Action:

Touch your forehead
with your index and
middle fingers.

January

duck
click
_ _nd
_ _sh
_ _sp
s_ _n
_ _tch
s_ _llow
May
June

‹wa› saying /wo/

Write some ‹wa› words in the swan.

May
M_y
_a_

June
J_n_
_u_e

Choose a word from the list to fit each sentence.

My _____ says two o'clock.

She was stung by a _____.

We must _____ our hands.

A _____ is a big, white bird.

Read these **nouns**, and give each **proper noun** a capital letter.

england

mrs swan

michael

monday

flower

wand

fire

dog

zack

september

chair

new zealand

mr brown

house

watch

hannah

Adjectives

Choose a name for a planet
and write it on the line.

Touch the side of your
temple with your fist.

_____

Imagine an alien living on the planet.
Write an **adjective** to describe the alien's head in the first box, and draw
the head next to it. Then do the same for the alien's body and feet.

My alien has a

(any adjective)

head...

...a

(texture adjective)

body...

...and some

(colour adjective)

feet!

19

thin
thick
t _ _ ch
y _ _ ng
d _ _ ble
tr _ _ ble
c _ _ ntry
n _ _ rish
July
August

‹ou› saying the /u/ sound

Write some ‹ou› words in the young birds.

Choose a word from the list to fit each sentence.

Is he from the town or the _____?

A kitten is a _____ cat.

Oh dear! We shall be in _____.

The oven is hot! Do not _____ it.

July
J _ l _
_ u _ y

August
A _ g _ s _
_ u _ u _ t

Write an **adjective** in each space.

I have a _____ dog with a _____ bark.

The _____, _____ child played football.

The tree was _____ and _____.

My hair is _____ and my eyes are _____.

20

Plurals: ‹-s› and ‹-es›

Draw more of each thing to make the pictures show plurals.
Write the plural **nouns** underneath.

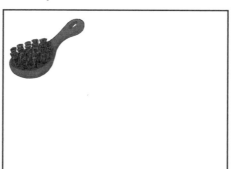

_____ _____ _____

_____ _____ _____

Write the word for each picture.

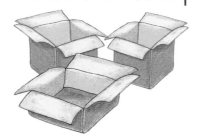

_____ _____ _____

_____ _____ _____

cliff

off

___

h___

p___

st___

ch___

h___brush

September

October

‹air› saying the /air/ sound

Write some ‹air› words in the hair.

Choose a word from the list to fit each sentence.

Her balloon floated up in the _____.

I brush my _____ with a _____.

The baby sits on a high_____.

He has a new _____ of shoes.

September

S_p_e_b_r

_e_t_m_e_

October

O_t_b_r

_c_o_e_

Give the plural for each of these **nouns** by adding ‹-s› or ‹-es›.

_____   _____   _____   _____

Possessive Adjectives

Match each pronoun to its **possessive adjective** and colour the **possessive adjectives** in blue.

| I | you | he | she | it | we | you | they |

| their | its | your | **my** | her | his | our | your |

Choose the right **possessive adjective** for each sentence.

They put on _____ coats.

I put on _____ coat.

He puts on _____ coat.

We put on _____ coats.

She puts on _____ coat.

You put on _____ coat.

You put on _____ coats.

Choose a **noun** for each **possessive adjective**.

my _____

your _____

his _____

her _____

its _____

our _____

your _____

their _____

Underline the **possessive adjectives** in blue.

Ben's friend, Sarah, came to visit. She brought her colouring books and pencils.

"Your books have lovely pictures in them," said Ben.

"This is my favourite book," replied Sarah. "If we share our coloured pencils, we will have plenty of colours for that picture."

Ben fetched his pencils. He took them out of their box.

buzz
fizz
e _ _ o
_ _ oir
_ _ emist
stoma _ _
_ _ ristmas
_ _ aracter
November
December

‹ch› saying the /k/ sound

Write some ‹ch› words in the choir.

Choose a word from the list to fit each sentence.

I sing in the _____.

December 25th is _____ Day.

She was ill with a _____ ache.

The _____ sells medicine.

November
N _ v _ m _ e _
_ o _ e _ b _ r

December
D _ c _ m _ e _
_ e _ e _ b _ r

Complete each sentence with a **possessive adjective**.

your   its   their   our   his   your   my   her

The children took out _____ pencil cases.

The boy read _____ book.

My sister played _____ recorder.

We sang _____ favourite song.

24

Homophone Mix-ups

Choose the right word to complete each sentence.

there or their ?

They put on _____ hats.

Leave the parcel over _____.

_____ he is, behind the tree.

The children rode _____ bikes.

_____ is no-one at home.

are or our ?

You _____ very tall.

_____ house has a red door.

They _____ all going to a party.

We put on _____ boots to go outside.

He likes _____ cat.

Write some more sentences containing there, their, are or our.

_____

_____

_____

_____

next
quit
m_k_
p_ _
m_ _n
cl_ _
w_ _st
r_ _nstorm
half
quarter

The /ai/ sound: ‹ai›, ‹ay› or ‹a_e›?

Underline the spelling you think is correct. Then use a dictionary to check your answer, and tick the right spelling.

wate
wait
wayt

ayt
ate
ait

day
dai
daye

name
naym
naim

traye
tray
trai

snake
snayk
snaik

Choose a word from the list to fit each sentence.

She made a model from _____.

Is it free, or do we have to _____?

I got wet in the _____.

My jeans have a tight _____.

half (½)
h_l_
_a_f

quarter (¼)
q_a_t_r
_u_r_e_

there or their?

_____ they are! Up _____.

_____ toys are over _____.

are or our?

We _____ going to visit _____ grandma.

They _____ all coming to _____ school.

26

A C Alphabetical Order

B

Write out the alphabet in the four groups.

1.___ ___ ___ ___   2._____

3.___ ___ ___ ___ ___   4.___ ___ ___ ___ ___ ___ ___

For each set of three, decide which word comes first (1st), which word comes second (2nd), and which word comes third (3rd). If the words start with the same two letters, remember to look at the third letter of each word.

shell	1st	hill		crisp	
shop	3rd	hive		cross	
ship	2nd	hidden		crab	

pet	rocket	tree
pen	roof	train
people	round	trick

march	eat	world
magpie	east	wood
make	each	wolf

drink	need	knee
dress	nest	knock
drum	next	knife

27

arm
shark
s _ _ n
thr _ _
s _ _ t
cr _ _ m
pl _ _ se
t _ _ nager
eleven
twelve

The /ee/ sound: ‹ee› or ‹ea›?

Underline the spelling you think is correct. Then use a dictionary to check your answer, and tick the right spelling.

bee
bea

leef
leaf

cheese
chease

streat
street

east
eest

dream
dreem

Choose a word from the list to fit each sentence.

I like strawberries and _____.

Eight plus _____ makes eleven.

We have _____ the new film.

_____ take care of my rabbit.

eleven (11)
e _ e _ e _
_ l _ v _ n

twelve (12)
t _ e _ v _
_ w _ l _ e

Which word would come 1st, which 2nd, and which 3rd in a dictionary?

green
grass   1st
grin

blue
black
block

smile
smell
small

skin
skunk
skate

allow
also
along

paper
paint
parrot

28

Are These Sentences?

Read each line. If there is a verb, underline it in red, and mark the sentence right with a tick. If there is no verb, mark the line wrong with a cross.

The ducks swim on the pond. ☐   The cat watches the birds. ☐

A spotty dog. ☐   The park keeper sweeps up the leaves. ☐

A wooden boat with a blue sail. ☐   The tall tree. ☐

A bird sings. ☐   A spotty dog has a stick in his mouth. ☐

The boys play bat and ball. ☐   The rabbit hides from the fox. ☐

Write some more sentences about the picture.

_____

_____

_____

REMEMBER A sentence needs to have a verb, as well as a capital letter at the beginning and a full stop at the end.

snug
flex
fl_ing
s___t
s_d_
d__
br___t
sunsh_n_
thirteen
fourteen

The /ie/ sound: ‹ie›, ‹igh›, ‹y› or ‹i_e›?

Underline the spelling you think is correct. Then use a dictionary to check your answer, and tick the right spelling.

bike
bighk
biek

ly
ligh
lie

sky
skigh
skie

ryd
ried
ride

bigh
by
bie

liet
light
lite

Choose a word from the list to fit each sentence.

They were _____ their kite.

Water the plant or it will _____!

The _____ is very bright.

I waved until she was out of _____.

thirteen (13)
t_i_t_e_
_h_r_e_n

fourteen (14)
f_u_t_e_
_o_r_e_n

Underline the verbs in these sentences in red.
There can be more than one verb in a sentence.

I fly my kite.

The big boat sails across the sea.

The dog barks and runs after the ball.

The children hop, skip and jump.

Adverbs

Think of an **adverb** to describe each **verb**.
Write the **adverbs** on the lines to complete your poem.

My Day

I wake _____,

I get out of bed _____,

I eat my breakfast _____,

I go to school _____,

I work _____,

I listen _____,

I play _____,

I speak _____,

I go home _____,

I watch television _____,

I wash _____,

I go to bed _____,

I sleep _____ and

I dream _____.

Illustrate two lines from your poem. Write the lines underneath.

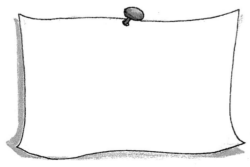

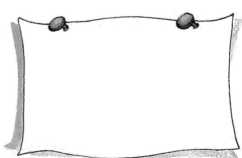

_____   _____

The /oa/ sound: ‹oa›, ‹ow› or ‹o_e›?

Underline the spelling you think is correct. Then use a dictionary to check your answer, and tick the right spelling.

such
luck
h_m_
fr_z_
f_ _l
st_n_
t_ _st
sn_ _ball
fifteen
sixteen

broak
browk
broke

towd
toad
tode

bloa
blow
blowe

nows
nose
noas

coste
cowst
coast

elboa
elbow
elbowe

Choose a word from the list to fit each sentence.

A _____ is a baby horse.

They ate buttered _____.

I went _____ after school.

We had a _____ fight.

fifteen (15)
f_f_e_n
_i_t_e_

sixteen (16)
s_x_e_n
_i_t_e_

Underline the verbs in these sentences in red.
Write an adverb on each orange line.

She sings _____.

He dresses _____.

The cat plays _____.

We cut out the pictures _____.

Verbs

'to be'

Action:

Move your arms back and forth at your sides, as if you are running.

Fill in the verb 'to be' in the present tense.

I _____   we _____

you _____   you _____

he/she/it _____   they _____

Write in the missing parts of the verb 'to be'.

You _____ very tall.

She _____ a girl.

Today, they _____ happy.

Ben said, "I _____ six years old."

The car _____ red.

We _____ in the race.

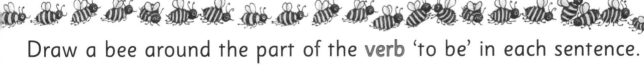

Draw a bee around the part of the verb 'to be' in each sentence.

It is a lovely day today.

She is in the choir.

The bees are busy.

The tree is tall.

"I am sorry," he said.

You are good at dancing.

sunk
book
h_g_
f_s_
resc__
que__
_ _e
_s_ful
seventeen
eighteen

The /ue/ sound: ‹ue›, ‹ew› or ‹u_e›?

Underline the spelling you think is correct. Then use a dictionary to check your answer, and tick the right spelling.

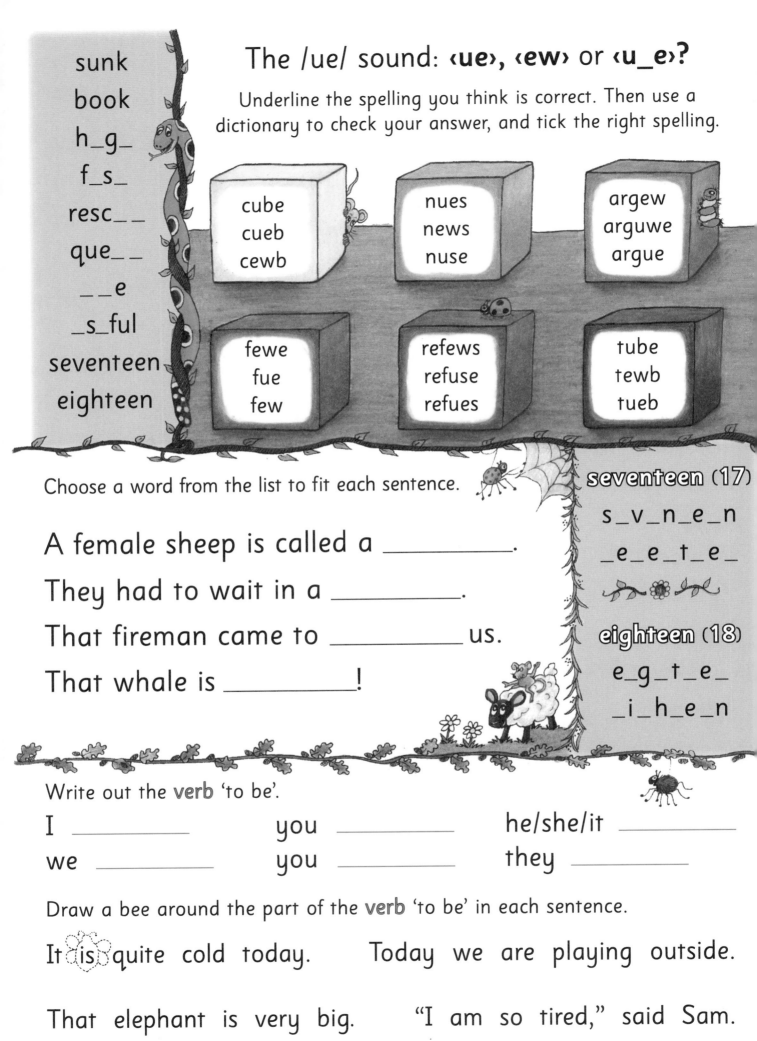

cube
cueb
cewb

nues
news
nuse

argew
arguwe
argue

fewe
fue
few

refews
refuse
refues

tube
tewb
tueb

Choose a word from the list to fit each sentence.

A female sheep is called a _____.

They had to wait in a _____.

That fireman came to _____ us.

That whale is _____!

seventeen (17)

s_v_n_e_n

_e_e_t_e_

eighteen (18)

e_g_t_e_

_i_h_e_n

Write out the **verb** 'to be'.

I _____   you _____   he/she/it _____

we _____   you _____   they _____

Draw a bee around the part of the **verb** 'to be' in each sentence.

It is quite cold today.   Today we are playing outside.

That elephant is very big.   "I am so tired," said Sam.

Vers

Regular Past Tense

Add the right **verb** ending to the **verb** root in each mouse.

Action:

Point backwards over your shoulder with your thumb.

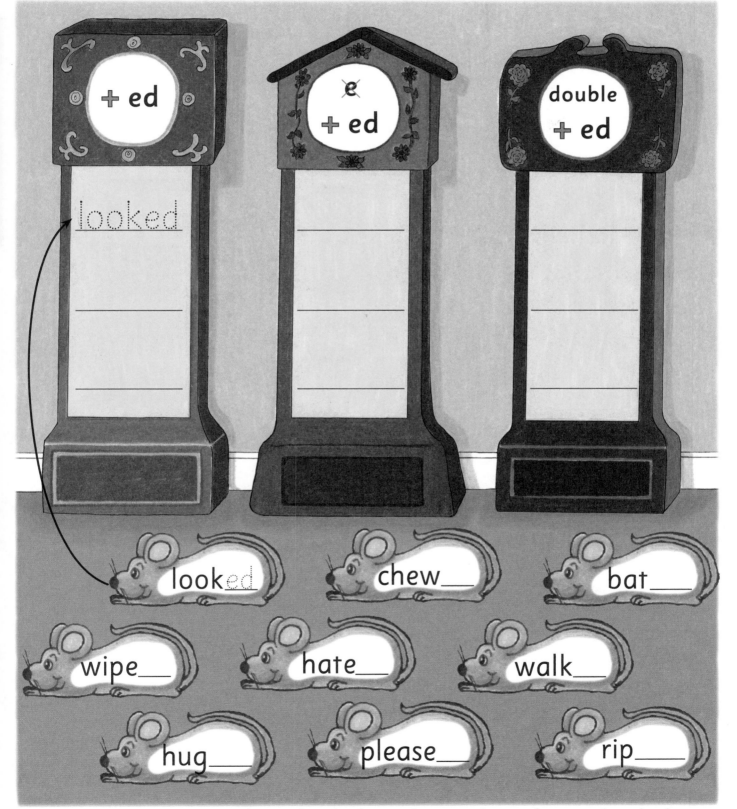

+ ed

e̶ + ed

double + ed

looked

looked   chew__   bat__

wipe__   hate__   walk__

hug__   please__   rip__

Now join each mouse to the right clock, and copy the **verb** into the clock case.

hoo_
for_
ba_ _
bri_ _
de_ _
flo_ _
stru_ _
ba_ _pa_ _
nineteen
twenty

nineteen (19)
n_n_t_e_
_i_e_e_n

twenty (20)
t_e_t_
_w_n_y

The /k/ sound: ‹k› or ‹ck›?

Underline the spelling you think is correct. Then use a dictionary to check your answer, and tick the right spelling.

duck
duk

sack
sak

forck
fork

sharck
shark

oack
oak

chick
chik

neck
nek

boock
book

rocket
roket

bicke
bike

black
blak

cacke
cake

Underline the verbs in these sentences in red.
Then rewrite the sentences in the past tense.

I zip up my coat.
Yesterday, _____

He talks to his friend.
Last week, _____

Verbs

Irregular Past Tense

Not all **verbs** have ‹-ed› at the end in the past tense. Some **verbs** have irregular, or 'tricky pasts'.

e.g. **Today I** swim. ⟶ **Yesterday I** swam.

Match the present and past tenses of these **verbs**.

Present	Past
win	wrote
sing	won
drink	rode
get	dug
dig	drank
ride	sang
write	got

Now colour the pictures.

Rewrite these sentences in the past tense.

We sing a song. _____

He rides his bike. _____

I write a letter. _____

You win a prize. _____

The /er/ sound: ‹er›, ‹ir› or ‹ur›?

Underline the spelling you think is correct. Then use a dictionary to check your answer, and tick the right spelling.

drip
plug
th__d
wint__
b__d
ov__
h__t
butt__fly
th__ty
forty

gingir
gingur
ginger

pirple
purple
perple

girl
gerl
gurl

furst
ferst
first

bern
burn
birn

hirb
herb
hurb

Choose a word from the list to fit each sentence.

She fell and _____ her knee.

A _____ is a beautiful insect.

The snow was deep last _____.

I finished the race in _____ place.

thirty (30)
t_i_t_
_h_r_y

forty (40)
f_r_y
_o_t_

Each of these verbs has a tricky past tense. Write each past tense in the honeycomb.

run   sing   swim

dig   ride   win

Using a Dictionary

Use a dictionary to find out how each word should be spelt.
Write the word out correctly on the line, and illustrate the word in the box.

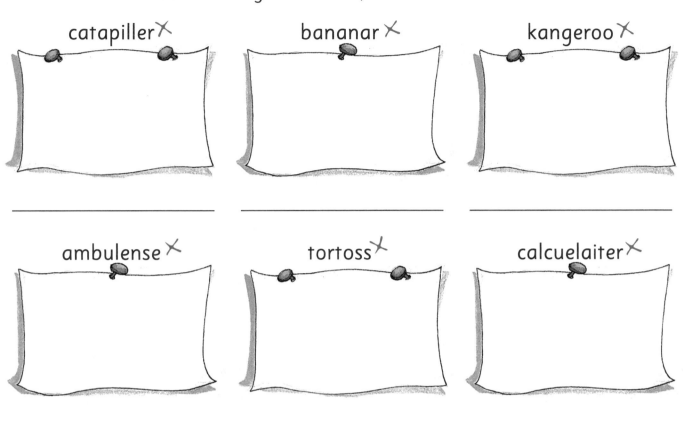

catapiller ✗

bananar ✗

kangeroo ✗

ambulense ✗

tortoss ✗

calcuelaiter ✗

Look up each word in the dictionary. Read the meanings, and illustrate each word.

hare

ocean

blizzard

dolphin

bungalow

aquarium

drag
trip
j_ _n
sp_ _l
p_ _nt
j_ _
r_ _al
_ _ntment
fifty
sixty

The /oi/ sound: ‹oi› or ‹oy›?

Underline the spelling you think is correct. Then use a dictionary to check your answer, and tick the right spelling.

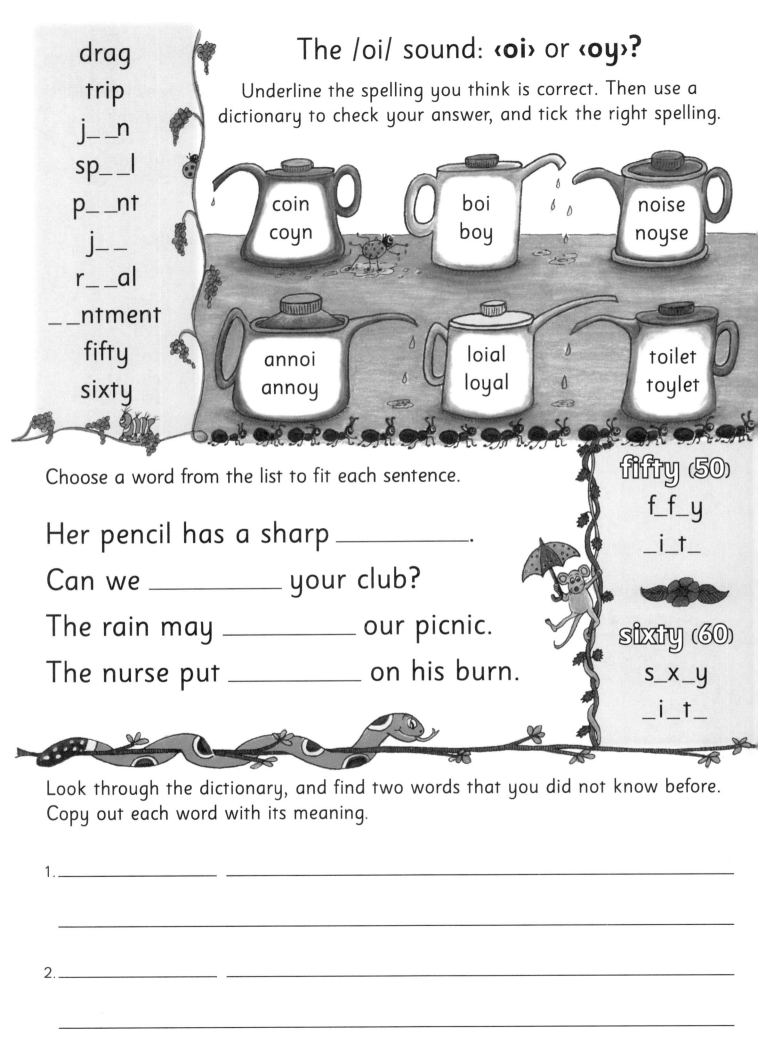

coin
coyn

boi
boy

noise
noyse

annoi
annoy

loial
loyal

toilet
toylet

Choose a word from the list to fit each sentence.

Her pencil has a sharp _____.

Can we _____ your club?

The rain may _____ our picnic.

The nurse put _____ on his burn.

fifty (50)
f_f_y
_i_t_

sixty (60)
s_x_y
_i_t_

Look through the dictionary, and find two words that you did not know before. Copy out each word with its meaning.

1._____ _____

_____

2._____ _____

_____

Proofreading Sentences

Proofread these sentences. Write out the correct spelling above each misspelt word and add in the missing punctuation.

1. Dolfins and wales live in the sea.

2. I saw some sheap with there lams on the hillsid.

3. it was mie berthday party

4. The dog ait the duc.

5. i wet on holiday with my muther father sister brother granma and grampa

6. Could I have a drinck pleas askt meg.

7. Whot is your naim sed the litle gerl.

8. Ouch i hit my thum wiv the hamer.

9. their are three yung Berds in the nest in are tree.

10. at the zoo we sor jiraffes elefants penguins and aardvarks.

Now colour the pictures.

snap
swam
l_ _d
cl_ _d
f_ _nd
n_ _
cr_ _d
sunfl_ _er
seventy
eighty

The /ou/ sound: ‹ou› or ‹ow›?

Underline the spelling you think is correct. Then use a dictionary to check your answer, and tick the right spelling.

out
owt

broun
brown

shout
showt

toun
town

mouth
mowth

croun
crown

Choose a word from the list to fit each sentence.

She grew a tall, yellow _____.

He _____ my lost watch.

A big _____ gathered to watch.

The music was very _____.

seventy (70)
s_v_n_y
_e_e_t_

eighty (80)
e_g_t_
_i_h_y

Proofread these sentences.

I have made a caik for yor berthday said mum .

Can you see the wite swon He asked .

the ducks kwacked lowdly as i threw them some bred .

She swimmed with dolfins last summir

Verbs

Action:

Move your arms back and forth at your sides, as if you are running.

'to be'

Conjugate the verb 'to be' in the present and past tenses.

Present

I _____

you _____

he/she/it _____

we _____

you _____

they _____

Past

I _____

you _____

he/she/it _____

we _____

you _____

they _____

Draw a bee around the part of the verb 'to be' in each sentence. Then rewrite each sentence in the past tense. Underline the past tense part of the verb 'to be' in red.

I ⌐am⌐ at school.

Yesterday _____

It is a beautiful sunny day.

Last Monday _____

We are happy.

Last week _____

They are good at football.

Last year _____

43

twig
from
t_ _ch
w_ _k
j_ _
n_ _th
str_ _
s_ _cepan
ninety
hundred

The /or/ sound: ‹or›, ‹al›, ‹au› or ‹aw›?

Underline the spelling you think is correct. Then use a
dictionary to check your answer, and tick the right spelling.

sor
sau
saw

forlt
fault
fawlt

tork
tauk
talk

storm
staum
stalm

borl
baul
ball

fork
fauk
fawk

Choose a word from the list to fit each sentence.

She always drinks through a _____.

We went for a _____ in the park.

He cooked rice in a big _____.

Shall we drive _____ or south?

ninety (90)
n_n_t_
_i_e_y

hundred (100)
h_n_r_d
_u_d_e_

Conjugate the verb 'to be' in the present and past tenses.

	Present	Past
I		
you		
he/she/it		
we		
you		
they		

Expanding a Sentence

① We can make a sentence more interesting by adding extra information to it. Read the simple sentence below. Underline the **noun** in black and the **verb** in red.

The dog barked.

② Now add an **adjective** to describe the **noun**.

Woof

The _____ dog barked.

③ Now add another **adjective**.

The _____ , _____ dog barked.

④ Now add an adverb to describe the verb.

WOOF!

The dog barked _____ .

⑤ Adding details can also make a sentence more interesting. What was the dog barking at?

The dog barked at _____ .

⑥ Now write out the sentence, adding in all the details.

The _____ , _____ dog barked _____

at _____ .

Now the sentence is much more interesting!

Expand these sentences on the lines.

The boy laughed.

_____

_____

The rabbit hopped.

_____

_____

45

film
kept
k _ _
hon _ _
mon _ _
donk _ _
chimn _ _
journ _ _
thousand
million

‹ey› saying the /ee/ sound

Write some ‹ey› words in the honey pot.

Choose a word from the list to fit each sentence.

She set off on a long _____.

He locked the door with his _____.

Bees collect pollen to make _____.

I saved up my _____ to buy a toy.

thousand
(1,000)
t _ o _ s _ n _
_ h _ u _ a _ d

million
(1,000,000)
m _ l _ i _ n
_ i _ l _ o _

Expand these sentences using **adjectives** and **adverbs**.

The _____ horse jumped _____

over _____

Our _____ cousin played _____

in the _____

Conjunctions

There are many conjunctions,
but these are six of the most useful ones.

Action:

and but because or so while

Hold out hands palm up.
Move both hands so one
is on top of the other

Underline the **conjunctions** in purple.

Would you like an apple or an orange?

I did not tell anyone the news because it was a secret.

He fell over but he did not hurt himself.

We played games while we waited.

cats and dogs

It rained so she took her umbrella.

Match each sentence part on the left to one on the right. Choose a **conjunction**
to join them together, and write it on the line.

I was late for school   _____ the band played.

We went to the country   _____ is it too late?

Kim ran fast in the race   _____ I overslept.

Is there time to play   _____ he ate some oats.

The horse was hungry   _____ had a picnic.

They listened quietly   _____ she did not win.

Choose a **conjunction** to complete these sentences.

The children hid _____ Dad counted to fifty.

Have you forgiven me, _____ are you still angry?

My feet were cold, _____ I put on my socks.

grip
milk

___
d___
y___
t___
sp___
___rings
zero
equals

‹ear› saying the /ear/ sound

Write some ‹ear› words in the earrings.

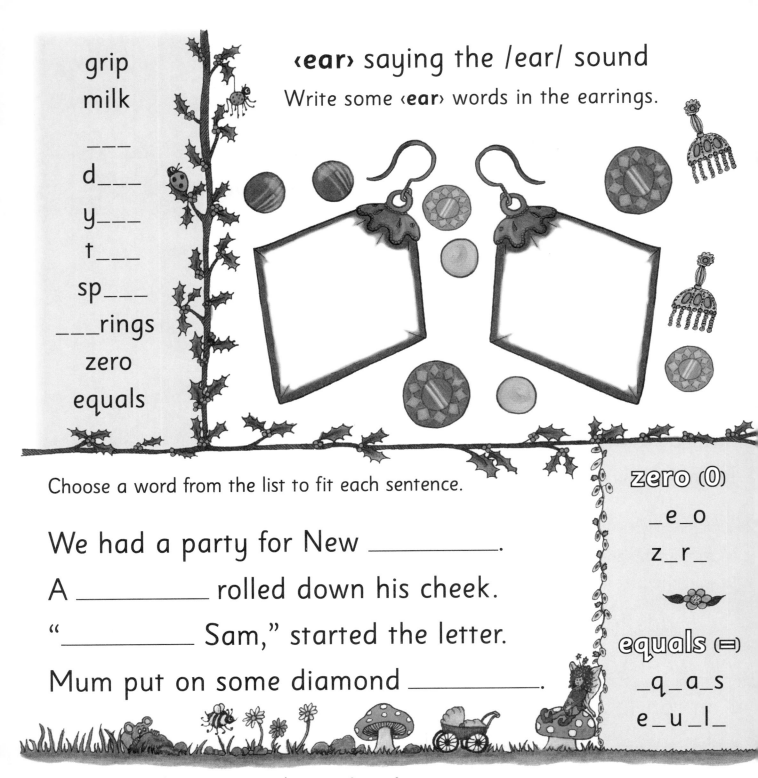

zero (0)
_ e _ o
z _ r _

equals (=)
_ q _ a _ s
e _ u _ l _

Choose a word from the list to fit each sentence.

We had a party for New _____ .

A _____ rolled down his cheek.

"_____ Sam," started the letter.

Mum put on some diamond _____ .

Complete each sentence with a **conjunction**.

and but because or so while

We went indoors _____ it started to rain.

I tried to catch the ball _____ I missed it.

Would you rather have cake _____ ice cream?

I would like apple pie _____ cream, please.

Plurals: ‹-s› and ‹-ies›

Write the plural for each word in the leaf. Then draw a picture for it in the daisy.

baby

monkey

daisy

fly

berry

donkey

boy

teddy

lady

belt
farm
_our
g_ost
r_yme
r_ythm
_onest
r_inoceros
centimetre
metre

Silent ‹h›

Write some silent ‹h› words in the rhinoceros.

Choose a word from the list to fit each sentence.

Poems often _____.

The train leaves in one _____.

I trust John because he is _____.

A _____ is a wild animal.

centimetre
c_n_i_e_r_
_e_t_m_t_e

metre
m_t_e
_e_r_

Each daisy has a **noun** in it. Write the plural of each **noun** on the leaf, and draw a picture in the daisy.

star

pony

toy

fairy

50

Word Webs

In the spaces of each word web, write some words that could be used instead of the word in the middle.

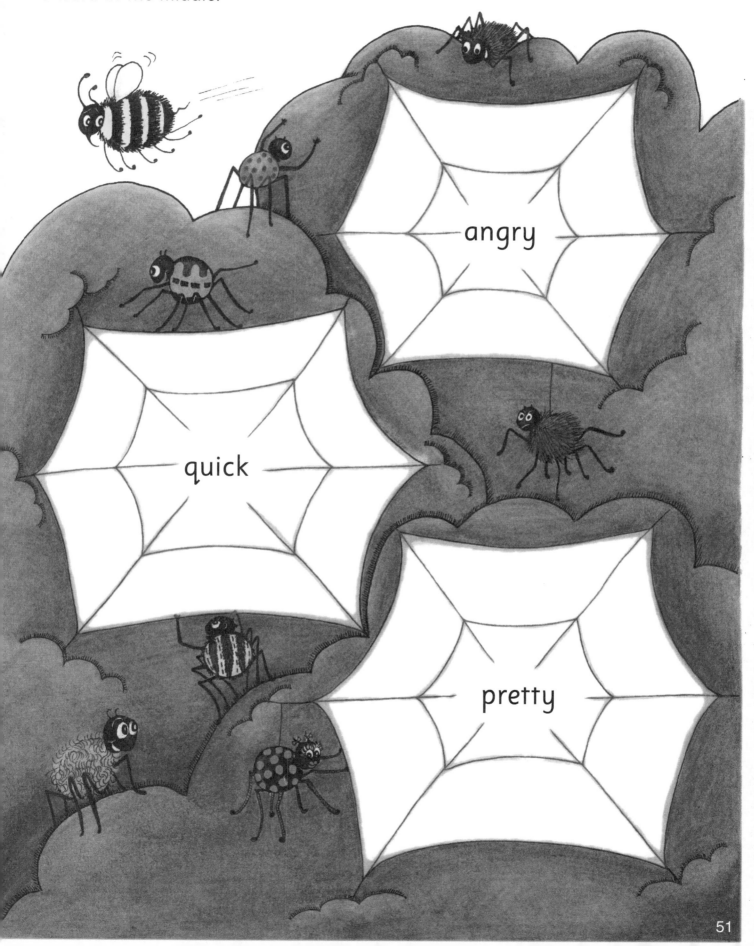

angry

quick

pretty

51

Silent ‹c›

Write some silent ‹c› words in the crescent moon.

land
quiz
s_ene
s_ent
mus_le
s_ience
s_issors
cres_ent
gram
kilogram

Choose a word from the list to fit each sentence.

The moon can be a _____ shape.

I cut the paper with my _____.

Those flowers have a lovely _____.

We do experiments in _____.

gram
g_a_
_r_m

kilogram
k_l_g_a_
_i_o_r_m

In the spaces in each word web, write some words that could be used instead of the word in the middle.

cold

happy

sad

52

Proofreading a Story

REMEMBER After writing something, it is a good idea to read it through to make sure there are no mistakes.

This is the beginning of a story. Read it through, correcting the spelling mistakes and adding in the punctuation marks and capital letters.

farmer brown has lots of animals on his farm he has rabits chickens cows horses a donkee and a goat the goat has a very bad temper and butts his horns against the tree trunc wen he is angry it wos munday morning and farmer brown was feding his animals good morning, he called to the horses here is your hai he gave the goat a big bag of oats just then a little robin flew down and started peking at them those are mine showted the goat

There are 13 missing capital letters, 9 missing full stops, 4 missing commas, 6 missing speech marks, 1 missing exclamation mark and 10 spelling mistakes! Snort!

What do you think might happen next? Continue the story on the lines.

_____

_____

_____

_____

_____

_____

_____

_____

kiln
wept
h____
c____
sh____
sc____
squ____
nightm____
millilitre
litre

‹are› saying the /air/ sound

Write some ‹are› words in the hare.

Choose a word from the list to fit each sentence.

Tim takes _____ of his pets.

We must _____ the sweets fairly.

A _____ is bigger than a rabbit.

She woke from a frightening _____.

millilitre
m_l_i_i_r_
_i_l_l_t_e

litre
l_t_e
_i_r_

Proofread this story.

the goat wos very angry that the robin had stolen sum of his brekfast he snorted and stamped his hooves the robin floo up into the oak tree and started singin the goat was so angry that he charged the tree Crash a larje branch fell on top ov him oh dear exclaimed farmer brown i shal have to go and get my tractor to get you owt.

Prefixes

There are many prefixes, but these are four of the most useful ones.

un- dis- mis- im-

Choose a prefix to go in front of each of the base words, and write it on the line. Then see how the meaning of the words and sentences has changed.

It was _____possible to walk along the path.

I really _____like writing stories in school.

Mum _____packed the holiday suitcases.

Jason _____understood what he had to do.

Choose a prefix to go in front of each of the base words in the fish bodies, and write it on the line in the fish's head.

You can use a dictionary to check whether you have chosen the right prefixes.

drip
silk
b____
t____
p____
w____
sw____
underw____
weight
volume

‹ear› saying the /air/ sound

Write some ‹ear› words in the bear.

Choose a word from the list to fit each sentence.

I shall _____ my new shoes.

The _____ was green and juicy.

Be careful not to _____ the paper!

I like to cuddle my teddy _____.

weight
w _ i _ h _
_ e _ g _ t
volume
v _ l _ m _
_ o _ u _ e

Make new words by joining up the prefixes and base words below.

tele-   tri-

scope   angle   cycle   vision

_____ _____ _____ _____

Apostrophe ‹s›

An apostrophe ‹s› shows that something belongs to someone.

Belonging Poem

Think of a person's name for each letter of the alphabet. Then think of something that the person might own, which begins with the same letter as their name.

REMEMBER Use an apostrophe ‹s› after each name to show that the next word is something belonging to that person.

Anna's apple,

Ben's book,

C

D

E

F

G

H

I

J

K

L

M

N

O

P

Quentin's

R

S

T

Usain's

V

W

Xander's

Y

Zoe's

57

must
stuck
na__on
sta__on
rela__on
ac__on
fic__on
dic__onary
minute
second

‹ti› saying the /sh/ sound

Write some ‹ti› words in the dictionary.

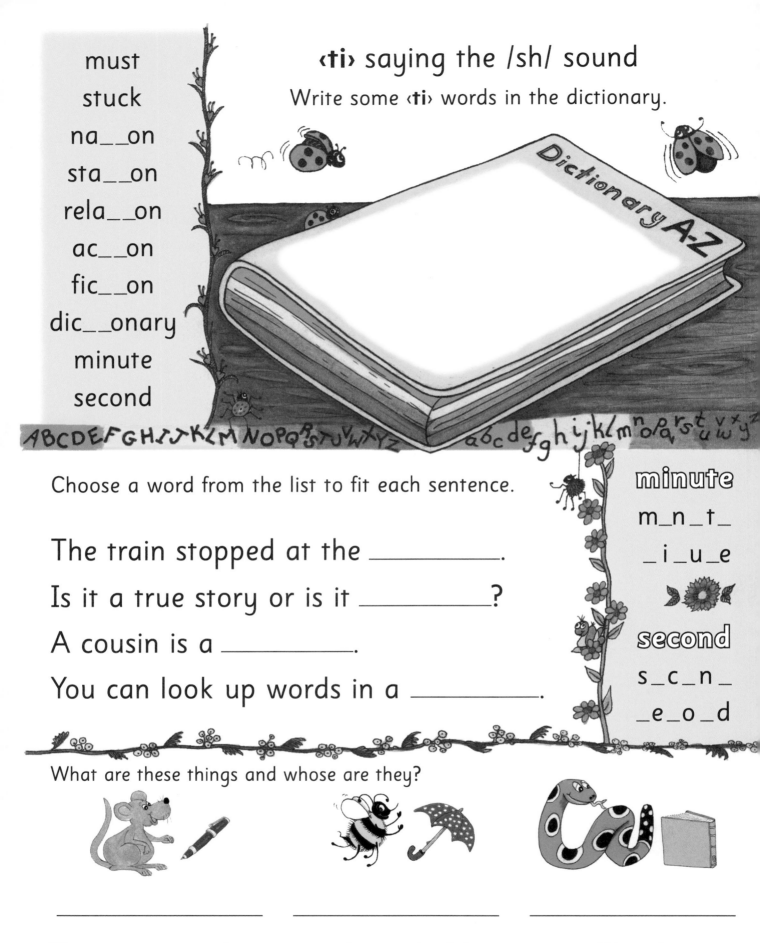

Dictionary A-Z

ABCDEFGHIJKLMNOPQRSTUVWXYZ   abcdefghijklmnopqrstuvwxyz

Choose a word from the list to fit each sentence.

The train stopped at the _____.

Is it a true story or is it _____?

A cousin is a _____.

You can look up words in a _____.

minute
m_n_t_
_i_u_e

second
s_c_n_
_e_o_d

What are these things and whose are they?

_____   _____   _____

There is an apostrophe ‹s› missing from each of these sentences. Write them in.

Bee went to Inky house on Saturday morning.
Inky liked Bee new red boots.

Contractions

We sometimes shorten pairs of words by joining them together and leaving out some of the letters. We use an apostrophe to show where the missing letter, or letters, used to be. These shortened words are called **contractions**.

Write out each contraction in full, as two words and with no letters missing.

couldn't _____ _____   didn't _____ _____

haven't _____ _____   mustn't _____ _____

don't _____ _____   I'm _____ _____

I shall I'll

Write out each pair of words as a contraction by joining them together and replacing some of the letters with an apostrophe.

I shall _____I'll_____   we shall _____

you will _____you'll_____   you will _____

he will _____   they will _____

she will _____

I'm winning!

it will _____

REMEMBER We use contractions when we speak. They should not be used in writing except when writing direct speech, or in a friendly note.

fist
best
occa__on
divi__on
revi__on
inva__on
explo__on
televi__on
fraction
estimate

‹si› saying the /sh/ and /zh/ sounds

Write some ‹si› words in the television.

Choose a word from the list to fit each sentence.

fraction
f_a_t_o_
_r_c_i_n

estimate
e_t_m_t_
_s_i_a_e

We watched a show on _____.

A wedding is a special _____.

There was a loud _____.

She can do multiplication and _____.

Write a contraction to complete the answer to each question.

"Is it raining?"
"No, it _____."

"Do you like mustard?"
"No, I _____."

"Did she telephone?"
"No, she _____."

"Could he swim?"
"No, he _____."

60

Prepositions

Choose a **preposition** to write in each gap. There can be more than one correct answer.

Action:
Point from one noun to another.

Inky's Journey

Inky left her mouse-hole and went...

_____ the path,

_____ the flowers,

_____ the fence,

_____ the garden,

_____ the field,

_____ the forest,

_____ the trees,

_____ the bridge and

_____ the farm.

across   near   among   into   from   towards   to

through   in   around   over   past   between

beside   down   under   along   round   up   behind

61

grub
slug
_____t
_____teen
_____ty
w_____
r__ndeer
n_____bour
child
children

‹ei› and ‹eigh› saying the /ai/ sound

Write some ‹ei› and ‹eigh› words in the reindeer.

Choose a word from the list to fit each sentence.

Four plus four equals _____.

Eight tens are _____.

She is our next-door _____.

A _____ has antlers.

child
c_i_d
_h_l_

children
c_i_d_e_
_h_l_r_n

Complete each sentence with a **preposition**.

   to   from   in   beside   up

I want to sit _____ my best friend.

Kayla climbed _____ the ladder.

We read _____ left _____ right.

Grandpa keeps his keys _____ his pocket.

62

Finding the Meaning

REMEMBER Homophones sound the same but have different spellings and meanings.

Use a dictionary to find out which word has which meaning. Write the meaning of each word on the line beside it.

beech _____

beach _____

flour _____

flower _____

right _____

write _____

wait _____

weight _____

whole _____

hole _____

meet _____

meat _____

sea _____

see _____

hear _____

here _____

Choose the correct word to complete each sentence.

where or wear ?

"_____ are we going?" asked Kelly.

I want to _____ my favourite sweater.

ark
clever
gl_ves
s_n
fr_nt
d_zen
m_nkey
s_mebody
woman
women

<o> saying the /u/ sound

Write some <o> words in the glove.

Choose a word from the list to fit each sentence.

There are twelve eggs in a _____.

I put on my hat, scarf and _____.

The _____ was swinging by his tail.

He has two daughters and a _____.

woman
w_m_n
_ o _ a _

women
w_m_n
_ o _ e _

to, too or two ?

I have _____ cats called Micky and Minnie.

We went _____ the mountains for our holidays.

There were _____ many of us _____ squeeze in the car.

I must go at _____ o'clock. Do you want to come _____?

64

Verbs

Suffixes: ‹-ing›

One of the most useful suffixes is ‹-ing›.
Make new words by adding ‹-ing› to the
verb roots, and write them on the lines.

-ing

Action:

Move your arms back
and forth at your sides,
as if you are running.

talk

_____

ride

_____

look

_____

run

_____

clap

_____

fly

_____

hope

_____

swim

_____

sneeze

_____

jog

_____

copy

_____

arrive

_____

shook
often
pic_____
fu_____
na_____
crea_____
frac_____
adven_____
mouse
mice

‹ture›

Write some ‹**ture**› words in the picture frame.

Choose a word from the list to fit each sentence.

mouse
m_u_e
_o_s_

mice
m_c_
_i_e

She painted a beautiful _____.

A dragon is a fantastic _____.

They had an exciting _____.

Tomorrow is in the _____.

Add the suffix ‹-ing› to each verb root, and write the new word on the line.

make _____   cook _____

stop _____   raise _____

jump _____   try _____

swing _____   whine _____

66

Comparatives and Superlatives

Suffixes: ‹-er› and ‹-est›

Two of the most useful suffixes are ‹-er› and ‹-est›.
Make **comparatives** and **superlatives** by adding ‹-er› and
‹-est› to the adjectives in Est-er Elephant and her friends.

quit
sweet
f__ld
p__ce
ch__f
th__f
sh__ld
bel__f
library
computer

‹ie› saying the /ee/ sound

Write some ‹ie› words in the shield.

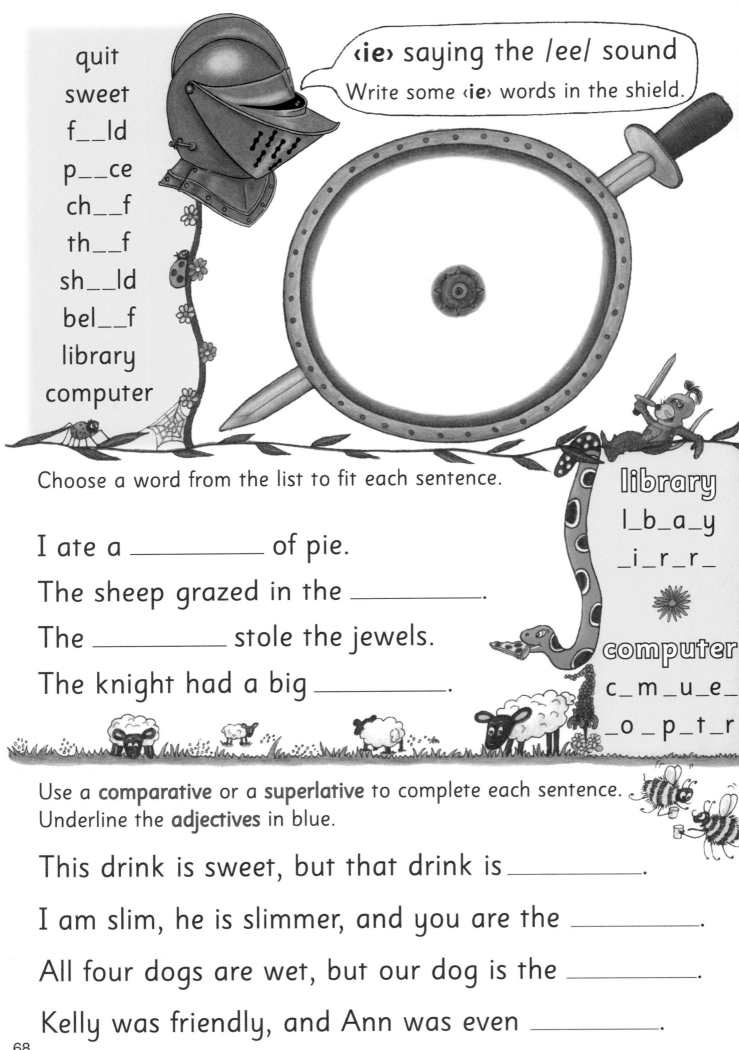

Choose a word from the list to fit each sentence.

I ate a _____ of pie.

The sheep grazed in the _____.

The _____ stole the jewels.

The knight had a big _____.

library
l_b_a_y
_i_r_r_

computer
c_m_u_e_
_o_p_t_r

Use a **comparative** or a **superlative** to complete each sentence.
Underline the **adjectives** in blue.

This drink is sweet, but that drink is _____.

I am slim, he is slimmer, and you are the _____.

All four dogs are wet, but our dog is the _____.

Kelly was friendly, and Ann was even _____.

68

Interesting Words

We use some words too often. Think of a more interesting word to replace each of the underlined words, and write it on the line. Use a different word in each sentence.

ran

The spider <u>ran</u> across the floor. _____

Tommy <u>ran</u> all the way home. _____

Their dog <u>ran</u> after our cat. _____

nice

It was a <u>nice</u> day. _____

We had a <u>nice</u> lunch. _____

Everyone was very <u>nice</u> to me. _____

good

The adventure park was <u>good</u>. _____

The rides were <u>good</u>. _____

I had a <u>good</u> time. _____

said

"Sh! The baby is asleep,' <u>said</u> Dad. _____

"Stop!" <u>said</u> the policewoman. _____

"Come over here," <u>said</u> the boys. _____

get

I want to <u>get</u> new shoes. _____

Please <u>get</u> me a glass of water. _____

They will <u>get</u> angry. _____

swung
spring
m____
w____
st____
sn____
bef____
seash____
English
language

‹ore› saying the /or/ sound

Write some ‹ore› words in the seashore.

Choose a word from the list to fit each sentence.

She _____ a blue coat yesterday.

Please may we have some _____?

I found a jellyfish on the _____.

Did he arrive _____ or after you?

English
E_g_i_h
_n_l_s_

language
l_n_u_g_
_a_g_a_e

Think of a more interesting word to replace each of the underlined words, and write it on the line.

She wore a <u>red</u> dress. _____

The dinosaur gave a <u>loud</u> roar. _____

It was a <u>cold</u> morning. _____

He caught a <u>small</u> fish. _____

Commas in Speech

REMEMBER A comma is needed between the spoken words and the rest of the sentence.

Add the missing commas and speech marks to these sentences.

1. My favourite colour is blue said the little girl.

2. The policewoman put her hand up and said Stop!

3. Hello said Uncle John. How are you today?

4. I know the names of all the dinosaurs said Toby and I've got a book about them at home.

REMEMBER A new line is needed each time someone different starts to speak.

Read this conversation, and rewrite it correctly underneath.

Hello Bee called Inky. Hello Inky replied Bee, waving her antenna and flying over to her friend. Did you have a good time at the adventure park yesterday? asked Inky. Oh yes sighed Bee it was brilliant. I went on all the rides and we stayed all day. Did everyone from the hive go? wondered Inky. Yes said Bee and then she paused. Everyone who wanted to she corrected herself.

_____

_____

_____

_____

_____

_____

_____

_____

_____

damp
stand
app_ _
tab_ _
litt_ _
midd_ _
bott_ _
syllab_ _
continent
world

‹le›

Write some ‹le› words in the apple.

Choose a word from the list to fit each sentence.

He asked for a _____ of lemonade.

My _____ sister is only two.

She laid the _____ for dinner.

I baked an _____ pie.

continent
c_n_i_e_t
_o_t_n_n_

world
_o_l_
w_r_d

Fill in the missing punctuation marks.

☐Do you want to come and play at my house☐☐ asked Josh☐

Tammy replied☐ ☐I☐ll have to ask my dad first☐☐

☐Look☐☐ exclaimed Josh☐ ☐There is your dad now☐ Why

don☐t you ask him☐☐

☐I will☐☐ Tammy agreed☐

72

Parsing

Identify as many of the different parts of speech as you can, and underline them in the correct colours.

Nouns   **Verbs**   **Pronouns**   **Adjectives**
Adverbs   **Prepositions**   **Conjunctions**

Inky's Necklace

It is a sunny morning. Inky and Bee are in the garden. Inky proudly shows Bee her birthday present, a silver chain. It glitters in the sunlight. Suddenly, a magpie swoops to the ground and grabs the chain.

"Stop!" shout Inky and Bee, but the naughty magpie escapes with it. Bee flies after the magpie. Inky runs quickly along the road below her friend. She follows the magpie and Bee into the forest. She sees Bee at the bottom of a tall tree.

"The nest is at the top of the tree," pants Bee. "I can't get the chain because the magpies are bigger than me." At this moment, an empty nutshell lands beside Inky.

"I am sorry!" calls a squirrel from the tree.

"It doesn't matter," Inky replies. "Could you help us?" She explains that the magpie took her chain. The squirrel scampers nimbly up the tree and fetches it from the nest.

Spellings

Spelling Test 1

1. _____

2. _____

3. _____

4. _____

5. _____

6. _____

7. _____

8. _____

9. _____

10. _____

Spelling Test 2

1. _____

2. _____

3. _____

4. _____

5. _____

6. _____

7. _____

8. _____

9. _____

10. _____

Spelling Test 3

1. _____

2. _____

3. _____

4. _____

5. _____

6. _____

7. _____

8. _____

9. _____

10. _____

Spelling Test 4

1. _____

2. _____

3. _____

4. _____

5. _____

6. _____

7. _____

8. _____

9. _____

10. _____

Spelling Test 5

1. _____

2. _____

3. _____

4. _____

5. _____

6. _____

7. _____

8. _____

9. _____

10. _____

Spelling Test 6

1. _____

2. _____

3. _____

4. _____

5. _____

6. _____

7. _____

8. _____

9. _____

10. _____

Spellings

Spelling Test 7

1.
2.
3.
4.
5.
6.
7.
8.
9.
10.

Spelling Test 8

1.
2.
3.
4.
5.
6.
7.
8.
9.
10.

Spelling Test 9

1.
2.
3.
4.
5.
6.
7.
8.
9.
10.

Spelling Test 10

1.
2.
3.
4.
5.
6.
7.
8.
9.
10.

Spelling Test 11

1.
2.
3.
4.
5.
6.
7.
8.
9.
10.

Spelling Test 12

1.
2.
3.
4.
5.
6.
7.
8.
9.
10.

Spellings

Spelling Test 13

1. _____
2. _____
3. _____
4. _____
5. _____
6. _____
7. _____
8. _____
9. _____
10. _____

Spelling Test 14

1. _____
2. _____
3. _____
4. _____
5. _____
6. _____
7. _____
8. _____
9. _____
10. _____

Spelling Test 15

1. _____
2. _____
3. _____
4. _____
5. _____
6. _____
7. _____
8. _____
9. _____
10. _____

Spelling Test 16

1. _____
2. _____
3. _____
4. _____
5. _____
6. _____
7. _____
8. _____
9. _____
10. _____

Spelling Test 17

1. _____
2. _____
3. _____
4. _____
5. _____
6. _____
7. _____
8. _____
9. _____
10. _____

Spelling Test 18

1. _____
2. _____
3. _____
4. _____
5. _____
6. _____
7. _____
8. _____
9. _____
10. _____

Spellings

Spelling Test 19

1. _____

2. _____

3. _____

4. _____

5. _____

6. _____

7. _____

8. _____

9. _____

10. _____

Spelling Test 20

1. _____

2. _____

3. _____

4. _____

5. _____

6. _____

7. _____

8. _____

9. _____

10. _____

Spelling Test 21

1. _____

2. _____

3. _____

4. _____

5. _____

6. _____

7. _____

8. _____

9. _____

10. _____

Spelling Test 22

1. _____

2. _____

3. _____

4. _____

5. _____

6. _____

7. _____

8. _____

9. _____

10. _____

Spelling Test 23

1. _____

2. _____

3. _____

4. _____

5. _____

6. _____

7. _____

8. _____

9. _____

10. _____

Spelling Test 24

1. _____

2. _____

3. _____

4. _____

5. _____

6. _____

7. _____

8. _____

9. _____

10. _____

Spellings

Spelling Test 25

1. _____
2. _____
3. _____
4. _____
5. _____
6. _____
7. _____
8. _____
9. _____
10. _____

Spelling Test 26

1. _____
2. _____
3. _____
4. _____
5. _____
6. _____
7. _____
8. _____
9. _____
10. _____

Spelling Test 27

1. _____
2. _____
3. _____
4. _____
5. _____
6. _____
7. _____
8. _____
9. _____
10. _____

Spelling Test 28

1. _____
2. _____
3. _____
4. _____
5. _____
6. _____
7. _____
8. _____
9. _____
10. _____

Spelling Test 29

1. _____
2. _____
3. _____
4. _____
5. _____
6. _____
7. _____
8. _____
9. _____
10. _____

Spelling Test 30

1. _____
2. _____
3. _____
4. _____
5. _____
6. _____
7. _____
8. _____
9. _____
10. _____

Spellings

Spelling Test 31	Spelling Test 32	Spelling Test 33
1.	1.	1.
2.	2.	2.
3.	3.	3.
4.	4.	4.
5.	5.	5.
6.	6.	6.
7.	7.	7.
8.	8.	8.
9.	9.	9.
10.	10.	10.

Spelling Test 34	Spelling Test 35	Spelling Test 36
1.	1.	1.
2.	2.	2.
3.	3.	3.
4.	4.	4.
5.	5.	5.
6.	6.	6.
7.	7.	7.
8.	8.	8.
9.	9.	9.
10.	10.	10.

ABCDEFGHIJKLMNOPQRSTUVWXYZ

Nouns
·A noun is something we can see, or hear, or touch.
·The colour for all types of noun is black.

Proper Nouns
·A proper noun is the name of a particular person, place, or thing.
·The action for a proper noun is to touch your forehead with your index and middle fingers.

Common Nouns
·A common noun is any noun that is not a proper noun.
·The action for a common noun is to touch your forehead with all the fingers of one hand.

Pronouns
·Pronouns are the little words used to replace nouns.
·The colour for all types of pronoun is pink.
·The actions for pronouns are:
> For **I**, point to yourself.
> For **you** (singular), point to someone else.
> For **he**, point to a boy.
> For **she**, point to a girl.
> For **it**, point to the floor.

For **we**, point in a circle, including yourself and others.
> For **you** (plural), point to two other people.
> For **they**, point to the next-door class.

Adjectives
·An adjective describes a noun or a pronoun.
·The action for an adjective is to touch the side of your temple with your fist.
·The colour for adjectives is blue.

Verbs
·A verb is a doing word.
·The action for verbs in general is to clench your fists and move your arms backwards and forwards at your sides, as if running.
·The colour for all types of verb is red.

Past Tense Verbs
·The action for the past tense is pointing backwards over your shoulder with your thumb.

Present Tense Verbs
·The action for the present tense is pointing towards the floor with the palm of the hand.

Verbs in the Future
·The action for verbs that describe the future is pointing towards the front.

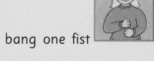

Adverbs
·An adverb describes a verb.
·The action for adverbs is to bang one fist on top of the other.
·The colour for adverbs is orange.

Conjunctions
·A conjunction is used to join parts of a sentence.
·The action for conjunctions is to hold your hands apart with palms facing up. Move both hands so one is on top of the other.
·The colour for conjunctions is purple.

Prepositions
·A preposition relates one noun or pronoun to another.
·The action for prepositions is to point from one noun to another.
·The colour for prepositions is green.